I0014489

PYTHON

FUNDAMENTAL HINTS AND TIPS TO KICK START YOUR PYTHON SKILLS

John McMurphy

Copyright © 2016 John McMurphy

All rights reserved

CONTENTS

Introduction

Congratulations on purchasing *Python: Fundamental hints and tips to kick start your python skills*. Thank you very much for your purchase! Python is used in just about every application that we use. As you move along in this book, you will gain a better understanding of how many of these applications actually work.

To ensure that you will have a complete understanding of Python, the following chapters will explain what Python is, and then take you step by step through the entire Python process. In this book, you will also learn tips and tricks that will help you to make your Python experience even better! Once you learn Python, there are no limits as to where you can go! It was designed to be fun for the programmer and easy to use. It was actually named for Monty Python so you can imagine the frame of mind that the originator was in at the time of conception. Once you learn Python, you will begin to build tools and prototypes rather fast. The tips and tricks that will be outlined in this book are geared to helping you get over any hurdles you may face and to give you a boost forward to help you to meet your objectives.

There are many books on Python on the market, so thanks again for choosing this one! I've made every effort to make sure that this book is as full of as much information as possible, so please enjoy!

Chapter 1: What is Python?

Python is a very much used programming language founded in 1990. Its name references the very funny British comedy group Monty Python. It is a favorite of programmers because it was designed to be all purpose, and its syntax allows the user to write their program in fewer lines of script then they would use in other programming languages such as Java. It is freely available and can make solving a computer problem easy as pie. You can write your code one time and then run it on almost any computer without having to make changes to the program. Python is not a compiled language rather, it is interpreted so it is converted to computer readable code at the time that it's ran and not before.

Python is used every day in Google, NASA, YouTube, the Government and many Non-Profit organizations. Python is also used in many on-line games. Especially the huge massive multiplayer games such as World of Warcraft. You would be able to use Python yourself for backend web development, data analysis, artificial intelligence, science, games, apps, etc.

If you are sitting there worried that you will need to be a math whiz to learn Python, then please relax. There is not a bunch of complicated math in programming. Programming doesn't actually require any math beyond the basics. And if you are good at solving Sudoku puzzles, you will be fine with programming. If you don't know what Sudoku puzzles are, I've included a picture below. On the left is the puzzle and on the right is another puzzle that has been solved.

Left (puzzle):

			8					
		3				4		
4		9	7		2		6	
	2				6			
5		3				4		8
			8				7	
6		8		4		5		9
	5				3			
			2					

Right (solution):

3	6	9	2	5	8	4	1	7
7	1	4	9	3	6	2	8	5
5	8	2	7	1	4	6	3	9
9	3	6	4	7	1	8	5	2
2	5	8	6	9	3	1	7	4
4	7	1	8	2	5	3	9	6
1	4	7	3	6	9	5	2	8
8	2	5	1	4	7	9	6	3
6	9	3	5	8	2	7	4	1

http://printablesudoku.blogspot.com

To solve a Sudoku puzzle, you must fill in the numbers 1-9 in each row, column, and each 3x3 interior square of the whole board. It is not difficult once you get the hang of it.

Chapter 2: Downloading Python

There are 3 Python versions that you can choose to download. You have the choice of downloading either, Windows, Mac, or Ubuntu Please visit http://python.org/downloads to download the program for free.

Please make sure that you download Python 3.4.0. That is the latest version and the version that we will cover in this book.

On the download page, you will find 64 bit and 32 bit installers. If you purchased your computer later than 2007, you will want the 64 bit version. If you purchased your computer prior to 2007, you will want the 32 bit version. If you want to be sure then follow these steps:

- If you are running windows, go to the start menu, click control panel, system and then check to see whether the system type says 32 bit or 64 bit.
- If you have an OS X system, go to the Apple menu, select About this Mac, then more info, system report and then hardware. Look at the processor name field. For a 32 bit computer, it will say Intel Core Duo or Intel Core Solo. If the label says Intel Core 2 Duo or anything else, then it is a 64 bit computer.
- If you have a Ubunto Linux system, then the procedure would be to open a terminal and use the command uname –m. If you see a response of i686, that means you are operating a 32 bit machine and if you see x86_64, that means you are operating a 64 bit machine.

Now that you have figured out 32 bit vs. 64 bit, it's time to download the software. We will again go through the three systems. I want to cover all three just in case. I cannot assume that everyone is running windows or that everyone is running an Apple system.

WINDOWS

The file name for the download will end with .msi. Double click that file to download the Python installer. Then follow the instructions that you see:

- Install for all users, Next
- Install to C:\Python34 folder then click next
- Then click next again so you skip customization.

Mac OS X

Download the file ending in .dmg that is for your version and double click it. Then all you have to do if follow the instructions on the screen:

- Double click the Python.mpkg file. The admin password may be required.
- Click continue through the welcome section ad click agree.
- Select your hard drive name and click install. It may be called HD Macintosh.

UBUNTU

Python may be installed from the terminal if you follow these steps:

Enter sudo apt-get install python3

Enter sudo apt-get install idle3

Enter sudo apt-get install python3-pip

IDLE

When it's time for you to actually run programs, you will use Python Interpreter. However, the software where you will actually enter your programs is much more like word and is called IDLE or interactive development environment software. Again using the three possible systems you could be using, let's walk through the process of starting IDLE.

- If you are using Windows 7 or newer, click start, when the search box comes up enter IDLE, and then select it.
- If you are using Windows XP, click start, then select programs, then Python 3.4. Then click IDLE.

- On a Mac system, open Finder, click on Applications, Python 3.4 then click IDLE.

- If you are using Ubuntu, go to Applications, then Accessories, Terminal and enter idle3.

Interactive Shell

When you first open IDLE, your screen should be blank with the exception of some text that will look like this:

Python 3.4.0 (v3.4.0 : 04f714765c13, Mar 18 2014, 18:32:45) [MSC v.1600 32 bit (AMD32)] on win32Type "copyright", "credits" or "license ()" for more information.

The screen will be like this no matter what operating system you are running. This area where you will type your instructions into the computer is referred to as the shell, or interactive shell. It is similar to the Terminal on an Apple system or Command Prompt on a Windows system. This Interactive Shell (IDLE3) in Python allows you to enter code for Python to run all at one time as a program. As you type the instructions, the computer will read them and run them immediately. If you were to go to the interactive shell and type next to the >>> prompt:

>>> print ('Good Morning!') Then press Enter.

Immediately the shell should give you this response:

>>>print ('Good Morning!')

Good Morning!

Chapter 3: Entering into IDLE

Before using Python, you will need to learn some basic programming functions. In this chapter, we will go over some examples to help you learn to type into IDLE (the shell) and to learn more about how executing Python instructions will show you results instantly. You can enter these into your Python program as practice.

Entering your Expressions into the Interactive Shell

Go ahead and launch IDLE for your particular operating system as discussed in the last chapter.

Now you should see your window prompt. You should see this:

>>>

Go ahead and enter 5 +5 and Python should do some simple math.

>>> 5 + 5

10

The IDLE window should now look like this:

Python 3.3.2 (v3.3.2:d047928ae3f6, Oct 13 2016, 00:08:30) [MSC v.1600 64 bit (AMD64)] on win32

Type "copyright", "credits" or "license ()" for more information.

```
>>> 5 + 5

10

>>>
```

In Python, the text that you enter after >>> is called an expression. In this example the expression was 5 + 5. It is the most basic of programming instructions. Expressions consist values (5) and operators (+) and they always end up as a single value. Expressions can be used in Python code anywhere that you also would want to use a value.

For example; in our exercise, the 5 + 5 was evaluated to a single value of 10. A single value without operators an express could also be an expression, even though it is only evaluating itself.

```
>>> 10

10
```

If you make errors as you go along, it is okay! Everyone gets scared when a program crashes on their computer. Or their computer crashes. When this happens, it simply means that a program has stopped running unexpectedly. And that is because the computer is trying to read a code that it doesn't understand. So, if you write a code that Python can't understand, it will show you an error message and let you know.

If you aren't sure about the error message that Python gives to you, you can google the specific error message online and it will give you more specific information regarding that error.

Here is a table of the math operators in Python. They are listed from the most important to least important.

**   Exponent

     1 ** 4   6

%   Modulus/Remainder

     44 % 6   2.64

//   Integer division/floored quotient   33 // 5   6

/   Division

     33 / 5   6.6

*   Multiplication

     6 * 3   18

-                  Subtraction

     6 − 3   3

+   Addition

     5 + 5   10

Precedence in Python (the order of mathematics) is the same as regular math. The ** operator would be first in line and then * and on and on. All of the operations in Python are ran from the left to the right. If you want to change the usual order, you can certainly do that by using parentheses. Here are some that you can practice:

>>> 5 + 3 * 4

32

>>> (5 + 3) * 4

32

>>> 568432 * 32451

1.844618683

>>> 3 ** 6

216

>>> 32 // 8

4

>>> 22 % 6

1.32

>>> (6 − 3) * ((5 + 1) / (4 − 1))

12.0.

In each of these examples, you must enter the math, but Python will do the hard work and figure it out down to a single value.

It is very important for you to study this and know how this works since it is a fundamental part of Python.

If you are ever wondering if one of your instructions will work, simply enter it into the shell. Please don't fear making an error. You won't hurt anything. Not the program and not your computer. Python will just show you and error message to let you know that it doesn't understand.

Integers, Floating-Points and Strings

The name of a category for values is a Data Type. The three most common Data Types in Python are Integers, Floating-Points and Strings. Some of us will feel a bit like we are going back to math class here. But remember, it is just the basics. Let's break down the three Data Types.

Integers: These are whole numbers. For example; 2, 3, 10, 12, 15, 20, 25, etc. Basically, integers are any number without a decimal point.

Floating-point Numbers: These are any numbers that use a decimal point. That includes a number that would have a decimal point immediately after. The number 32. Is an example of a floating-point number. Other examples would be 1.5, 2.5, 1.25, 0.0, 0.5, 0.75, etc.

Strings: String are also called strs ("stirs"). When you are using strings, you will always surround them with a single quote so that Python knows where they begin and end. Or you can have a blank string which would be two single quotes without any characters in between them, like this ''. A good example of a string would be; ('Good Morning!') If you have entered a string and see the error message SyntaxError: EOL while scanning string literal, that means that you forgot the single quote mark at the end of your string. This is a common mistake many programmers make as they are going along, so just keep this error message in mind.

String Concatenation and Replication

We talked about operators and how they relate to math in Python. Now let's take a look at how operators work with strings.

String concatenation is using the + operator to join two strings together. Python actually allows you to omit this operator. But you should really understand how it works, because you most likely will want to use it. Here is what you would enter into Python to use this operator:

>>> 'Martha' + 'Greg'

'MarthaGreg'

Python takes the two values and evaluates them down to a single just like we saw in the math examples. Now, if you were to try combining an integer value and a string, Python wouldn't understand and you would receive an error message. You would see this:

>>> 'Martha' + 63

Traceback (It would show the last call):

File "<pyshell#26>", line 1, in <module>

'Martha' + 63

TypeError: Can't convert 'int' object to str implicitly

What this error message is saying is that Python thinks you are trying to add an integer to the string 'Martha'. Since Python can't convert data types automatically, then you will have to do this on your own, which we will take a look at a little further on when we are walking through our first program.

You can replicate a string by using the * operator. When you use a single string value and a single integer value, then using the * operator, it will multiply the string. For example:

>>> 'Martha' * 6

'MarthaMarthaMarthaMarthaMarthaMartha'

Although the ability to repeat things can come in handy, it is not used as often as concatenation. You can only use the * operator with two numeric values or with one string and one numeric value. If you try using it with any other combination, Python will just give you an error message.

Chapter 4: Python Practice Program

In this chapter we are going to create your first small program and then we will take it apart and look at it to show exactly how Python works with a simple practice program.

So far, we have been using the interactive shell to do our examples. The interactive shell is great for testing out instructions or inputting them on a time. However, when you write an entire program into Python, you will use the file editor. To open the file editor while in IDLE, go to File and then select new file.

You will see a window with a cursor. Just like in IDLE. This window will be different then the IDLE window because when you are typing in instructions, Python isn't going to run them right away. In Python, you are able to type in your entire program, then you are able to save the file and run the entire program at one time. Here's what the difference is between the windows:

- In the Python window you will see the >>> prompt.
- In the file editor, there will just be a cursor.

This is going to be an easy program that will say Nice Day and ask your name.

Try entering this into the window:

- # This program says Nice Day and askes about the weather
- print ('Nice Day!')
- print ('How is the weather')   # ask about the weather

- theWeather = input ()
- print ('It is a beautiful day, ' + theWeather)
- print ('The length of the weather is:')
- print(len(theWeather))
- print ('How old is your dog?')   # ask for their dogs age
- dogAge = input ()
- print ('You will be' + str(int(dogAge) + 1) + ' in a year.')

When you are done, you can save your program if you want, so that you don't have to retype it when you go back into IDLE. Go to File, and then click on Save As, enter hello.py in the file name field and then you can save it. Whenever you write programs you should save them. That way if your power goes out or you have an issue with your computer, you have your code.

Now that you've saved your program, let's run it. You want to select run, then run module. Or you can just press your f5 key. You will need to run your program from the Python window and not from the IDLE window. When you run your program it will open in the IDLE window. It will look like this:

Python 3.3.2 (v3.3.2:d047928ae3f6, October 14 2016, 00:08:42) [MSC v.1600 64 bit

(AMD64)] on win32

Type "copyright", "credits" or "license()" for more information.

```
>>> ================= RESTART
======================

>>>

Nice Day!

How is the weather?

Great!

It is a beautiful day! Great!

The length of the weather is:

6

How old is your dog?

7

You will be 8 in a year.

>>>
```

When Python can't find anymore code to read, the program exits, or stops running. You can then close the window.

Keep your program open in Python and let's look closer at the code that you wrote and at the instructions that Python is using.

Comments

The very first line of code that you entered into Python was actually a comment. *#This program says hello and asks for my name.* Comments can be used during your code to leave notes to yourself about what you are trying to have the code do. Python ignores these comments so don't worry that they are going to show as errors because they won't. Use the # (hash mark) and then write your comment.

Sometimes while writing code, programmers will use the hash tag to remove a line of code while they are testing a program. They call this commenting out code. If you are having difficulty with a program that isn't working then this can be a useful tool. Later you can take out the hash tag when you are ready to reinsert the line.

You can also add blank lines in between your code to make it easier to read. Python will also ignore these. You can then make your code more like reading a book and insert blank lines in between sections of code.

Print()

Using print() tells Python, the display the string value inside of the parentheses. For example, when you enter *print ('Hello world!')*, Python knows that your command is to display the words 'Hello world!' on the screen. Python does not print the quotes on the screen when it displays the text. The quotes tell Python where the start of the string (the text) is and where it ends.

Another useful function of print () is to leave a blank line in your program. You simply enter print () and enter then move onto your next line of code.

Input()

This function is used when you want to prompt the user to type information onto the screen and then press enter. For example, in our program, we used the code *myName = input()*.

Using the equal sign, assigns the myName variable to what the user enters (the input() variable). Then Python knows that whatever the user has entered is equal to myName in the code. If they entered Jenny as in our example, then the expression would equal to myName = Jenny.

Printing your Name

When we use the word print we are telling Python to print what is in the parentheses onto the screen. For example, we used print ('The weather is beautiful,' + theWeather) in our code. So we told Python to print on the screen, 'The weather is beautiful! Great!'. Using the + followed by theWeather told Python to add the weather to the text. You can also use this to print your name. In that instance, instead of inserting theWeather into the code, you would insert myName.

Len()

The Len() function calculates the number of letters that you are using in a string. The code in our program that we used was:

Print ('The length of the weather is:')

Print (len(theWeather))

From that code, Python knew to add the letters in your name and tell you how many there are. Go into the shell and try this:

>>> len ('I'm very sorry to hear that.')

22

>>> len (")

0

STR(), INT() and FLOAT().

If you want to concatenate a number like 63, you would use a string to get to print (). You would have to get the string value of '63".

So, you would type this code:

>>> str (63)

'63'

>>> print ('I am' + str(63) + 'years old.')

I am 63 years old.

All three of these functions work identical to each other. They take a value of a different type and then turn it into their own data type to get whatever type of data you need to work with.

You would use str () to concatenate a floating-point or an integer to a string. You would use int () to take an integer in string value and make it an integer value Note: input() will always return a string even if the user enters a number. The value of that number will then be a string.

Python will display the following error message if you are trying to use the int () function to give it a value to convert that it can't figure out is an integer:

>>> int('99.99')

Traceback (Always the last call):

  File "<pyshell#18>", line 1, in <module>

    int('99.99')

ValueError: invalid literal for int() with base 10: '99.99'

>>> int('twelve')

Traceback:

  File "<pyshell#19>", line 1, in <module>

    int('twelve')

ValueError: invalid literal for int() with base 10: '12'

You can also use the int () function to round floating-point numbers down. Likewise, if you would want to then round floating-point numbers up, you would just add a 1 to it afterward.

>>> int (9.9)

9

>>> int (9.9) +1

10

In our practice program, we used int () and str () at the end to get the value of the correct data type for our code. Here is the code we typed:

print ('What is the age of your pet')   #ask for their pet's age

petAge = input ()

print ('Your pet will be' + str(int(petAge) +1) + 'in a year.')

We entered 7 for our age. Since input() is always a string, you use int (myAge) to turn the value of 7 from a string into an integer so that Python can do the math to add one year (+ 1). Using str () converts the integer 7 into string form so that you can consternate it using the second string and then create the final message to be displayed.

Chapter 5: Python Dictionaries

Dictionaries, also called mappings, are Python data type used to store key value pairs. They allow you to easily , add, remove, find, or change values using keys. Unlike when you use a list, the information in Python dictionaries has no order. You can enter the key pairs in any order into the dictionary. Keep in mind not to use a for code when searching in the dictionary.

Creating a Dictionary

You can create a dictionary using a pair of curly braces ({}). All of the items in the dictionary will be made up of key, and then followed by a colon, which will then be followed by a value. Each item will be separated with commas. Try this:

friends = {

'Mary' : '111-222-333',

'Joseph' : '666-33-111'

}

In the example below, friends is the name of a dictionary with two items in it. Mary and Joseph are the two items in the dictionary. Each key that you use in the dictionary must be special.

An empty dictionary can also be created. If you were to create one, it would simply look like this:

>>> dict_emp = {}

Retrieve, Modify, and Add Elements

You can retrieve things from the dictionary using the following code:

```
>>> dictionary_name['key']
```

```
>>>friends ['Joseph']
```

'111-222-333'

If you have put that key into the dictionary, Python will return the value. If not, then you will see and error message of KeyError.

If you want to add or modify something in the dictionary, you would use the following code:

```
>>> dictionary_name['newkey'] = 'newvalue'
```

```
>>> friends['joe'] = '888-999-666'
```

```
>>> friends
```

```
{'joseph': '111-222-333', 'joe': '888-999-666', 'mary': '666-33-111'
```

If Python finds the key then it will be deleted. If not, the error message KeyError will be shown.

Looping Items

You can use the loop commands to get around elements in the dictionary. Here is an example:

```
>>> friends = {

... 'joseph' : '111-222-333',

... 'mary' : '666-33-111'

...}

>>>

>>> for key in friends:

... print(key, ":", friends[key])

...

joseph : 111-222-333

mary : 666-33-111

>>>
```

Using Len ()

You can also use the len () in the dictionary to see how many items are in a specific dictionary. You would something like this:

```
>>> len(friends)
```

2

This tells you that there are two items in the friends'
dictionary. The items we have in there are Mary and Joseph
from our examples.

In or Not in

If you are trying to see if a key is in a dictionary, you can use
the in or not in operators. If you wanted to check to see if
Mary was in the friends' dictionary, for example, you would
enter:

>>> 'mary' in friends

True

This would show that Mary is in the friends' dictionary.

You could also ask if Mary is not in the friends' dictionary
and that would look like this:

>>> 'mary' not in friends

False

Python would then answer false because Mary is in the
friends' dictionary.

Get ()

Always checking to see whether a key is in a dictionary can be tedious. Python has the get () method for it's dictionaries. In this method, Python uses a value key to find and a fallback to return if the key you searched for doesn't exist. Here is an example of wine not being in the Daytrip dictionary:

>>> Daytrip = {'plates': 5, 'glasses': 2}

>>> 'I have brought ' + str(daytrip.get('cups', 0)) + ' glasses.'

'I have brought 2 glasses.'

>>> 'I have brought ' + str(daytrip.get('wine', 0)) + ' wine.'

'I have brought 0 wine.'

Since there is not a wine key in the dictionary called Daytrip, the get () returns the default value 0. If you didn't use the get () method, then there would have been an error message. The error message would have looked like this:

>>> Daytrip = {'plates': 5, 'glasses': 2}

>>> 'I have brought ' + str(daytrip['wine']) + ' wine.'

Traceback (most recent call last):

  File "<pyshell#34>", line 1, in <module>

    'I have brought ' + str(daytrip['wine']) + ' wine.'

KeyError: 'wine'

Setdefault ()

If a key does not have a value in a dictionary then you will have to set one. The code you would normally use takes up to three lines and looks something like this:

```
spam = {'name': 'Daniel', 'age': 16}

if 'breed' not in spam:

spam['breed'] = 'Standardbred'
```

This method gives you a simpler way of setting a value using only a single line of code. The key you are checking for is the first argument that is passed to the method. Then if the key doesn't exist, the value to set at that key is the second argument passed. As long as the key is there, the setdefault () method will then return the key's value. Here is an example:

```
>>> spam = {'name': 'Daniel', 'age': 16}

>>> spam.setdefault('breed', Standardbred')

'Standardbred'

>>> spam

{'breed': 'Standardbred', 'age': 16, 'name': 'Daniel'}

>>> spam.setdefault('breed', 'ThororghBred')

'Standardbred'
```

>>> spam

{'breed': 'Standardbred', 'age': 16, 'name': 'Daniel'}

The dictionary in spam changes to { 'breed' ; 'Standardbred', 'age'; 16, 'name'; 'Daniel'}, the first time that the setdefault is called. The method will go back to the same value 'Standardbred' since this is now the default value set for the key 'breed'. The value for the key spam.setdefault ('breed', 'ThoroughBred') will not be changed when it is called next, because spam already has a set key named 'breed'.

To ensure that a key is there, the setdefault () method is great.

Built in Dictionary Methods

There are several built in methods for working in Python dictionaries. Here are a few of them and what they do:

popitem (): This randomly returns select items from the dictionary and removes the selected items.

clear (): This function deletes everything from the dictionary

keys (): This returns keys in dictionaries as tuples

values (): This function returns values in dictionaries as tuples get(key): If the key you are looking for isn't found, it will return None instead of giving you an error message.

pop(key): This method removes an item from the dictionary. It the key you want to remove is not found, you will see an error message.

Chapter 6: Python Functions

We have taken a look at the print (), input () and len ()
functions. Python offers several built in functions like these.
But, there are also functions that you can write on your own
and that is what we are going to talk about here in this
chapter.

To help you get a better idea of how functions really work,
let's practice creating one. Go to the file editor, and type this
small program in. Then save it as MyFunc.py:

1. def hello () :
2.   print ('Howdy!')
3.   print ('Howdy!!!')
4.   print ('Hello there.')
5. hello()
6. hello()
7. hello()

The first line that you typed is a defining statement. The def
statement defines the function named hello (). The next 3
lines of script are the main part of the function. Python will
run the function when it's first called and not when it's first
defined.

The last three hello lines or codes are called the function calls.
A function call is simply the function name and then ().
When Pythons execution gets to these last three lines of code
or the function calls, it will begin running the code there.
When it gets to a functions end, it will go back to the line that
started the function and continue going over the code.

In our program, the program calls hello () 3 times. When you run the program, it should look like this:

Howdy!

Howdy!!!

Hello there.

Howdy!

Howdy!!!

Hello there.

Howdy!

Howdy!!!

Hello there.

One of the major purposes here is for these functions to gather together code that gets executed more than one time. If you weren't able to accomplist that, you would have to reenter your code every time, and it would end up like this:

print ('Howdy!')

print ('Howdy!!!')

print ('Hello there.')

print ('Howdy!')

print ('Howdy!!!')

print ('Hello there.')

etc.

It is a good idea to avoid duplicating code. If you would ever want to update it, or have to fix it somewhere, then you would be replacing it everywhere you copied it.

Defining Statements with Parameters

As you are using the print () and len () functions, you will enter values (arguments) into the parentheses. Here, we will talk about how you can create your own unique functions that will take arguments without error.

Go ahead and Enter this sample program into the interpreter and then save it as myFunc2.py:

1. def hello (name) :
2. print ('Hello' + name)
3. hello ('Mary')
4. hello ('Jack')

Go ahead and run your program. You should see this:

Hello Mary

Hello Jack

The parameter is called name (the first code). A parameter is defined as a variable that stores an argument when a function is ran. When Python runs the hello () function for the first time, it is using the argument Mary (the third code). The program runs the function and will then automatically set the variable to 'Mary', which is what then will get printed by the print() statement (the second code).

The value stored in parameters becomes forgotten by Python when the function comes back. So, if you add the function print (name) after the hello ('Jack') function in the program we did before, Python would give you the error message (NameError) since there isn't a variable named name. It was forgotten by Python after the function call hello ('Jack') came back, so print (name) would refer to a variable that isn't there anymore.

Statements and Return Values

If you are using len () and give it and argument like 'Howdy', the function call equates out to the integer value 5. That is the length of the string that you entered into it (Howdy). The return value of a function is the value that a function call equals to.

When you are creating functions using def statements, it can be specified what the return values should be with return statements. Return statements consist of the return keyword and the value or expression that you want the function to give.

When you are using a return statement that has an expression, the return value is what the expression will equate to. Let's go into Python and try another sample program. In this sample, we will try a function that will give us a different string depending on what value we enter as an argument.

```
import random
```

1. def getAnswer (answerNumber):
2. if answerNumber == 1:
3.   return 'It is certain'
4. elif answerNumber == 2:
5.   return 'It is for sure'
6. elif answerNumber == 3:
7.   return 'Yes'
8. elif answerNumber == 4:
9. return 'Cannot see through the mist'
10. elif answerNumber == 5:
11.   return 'Ask again later'
12. elif answerNumber == 6:
13.   return 'Think harder and repeat question'
14. elif answerNumber == 7:
15.   return 'Absolutely not'
16. r = random.randit (1,7)
17. fortune = getAnswer (r)
18. print (fortune)

This program will look familiar to some of you if not all. The first thing Python does in the program is to import the random module (first code). In the second code, the get answer function is defined. Since the get answer function is only being shown and it isn't actually being called, Python will skip the language in it. Python will move onto the random.randint () function (code number 17). This is being asked ran with multiple arguments, one and seven. This includes the one and the seven themselves. This value then becomes kept within a variable named r.

The getAnswer (r) is called (code 18), and then Python goes back to the top of the getAnswer (r) function (code 3) and the value r becomes kept within a parameter called answerNumber. Depending on what the user choses as an answer, the function then will return to one of the many available string values. Then Python goes back to the code at the end that originally called getAnswer (r) (code 18). Then the string Python returns becomes given over to a variable we called fortune, then gets sent to a print (fortune) call (code 19). It is then entered onto the screen.

The None Value

In Pythons language, there is the None value which means the absence of value which is how it gets its name. When you are using the None value, you should always enter it using a capital N. This value can help you are storing something that can't get confused with real values in other variables.

Where programmers use None most often, is for what Python will return when you are using print (). Nothing needs to be returned to print (). It just displays the string on the screen. Unlike len () or input () which must have something return to them. However, since all function call must have a return value, print () uses None.

Using Keyword Arguments with Print ()

Arguments are usually defined by their place in the function call. You wouldn't get the same outcome from random.randint (3,8) as you would random.randint (8,3) Using random.randint (3,8) will result in a random number between 3 and 8. Using random.randint (8,3) will only cause an error message.

You can identify Keyword Arguments by the keywords used before function call in(). Programmers often use them for optional parameters. When using the print () function there are parameters end and separate that tell Python where to print text at the end of and in between arguments.

Here is an example:

If you enter this:

>>> print ('See you later")

>>> print ('alligator')

You would get this output:

See you later

Alligator

You would see the two strings on two separate lines since print () will automatically add a newline Character at the end of the string that has been passed. You do have the option of setting an end keyword argument. That would then change the string to a different string that would then appear on one line. You would then write the program like this:

>>> print ('See you later', end='')

>>> print ('Alligator')

Then your output would appear like this:

See you laterAlligator

Everything would then end up printed on one single line since there is not a new-line after 'See you later'. Instead, a blank string has been printed. If for some reason you would need to disable a newline this could be very useful to you.

Chapter 7: Exceptions and Errors

Up until now, we haven't really discussed errors that you may come across. You have seen a few mentioned in our examples, but let's take a closer look at them since you will no doubt encounter them.

Syntax Errors

Syntax errors are the most common and are also called parsing errors. A syntax error may look like this:

Syntaxerror: invalid syntax

This error message will then repeat the wrong line and display a very small arrow to show where the error was found. The error will have been caused by or Python will have detected it the space preceding the arrow. So you want to see what is going on in that space. Is something missing? Or maybe something is there that shouldn't be.

Exceptions

Even when statements and expressions are correct, they may still cause errors when there is an attempt to execute them. When errors are found during the running of a program, the are referred to as exceptions and they are not fatal. Most of the exceptions aren't handled by Python and then an error message will be shown.

Here is an example:

```
>>> 18 * (1/0)
Traceback (most recent call last):
File "<stdin>", line 1, in <module>
ZeroDivisionError: division by zero
>>> 6 + spam*3
Traceback (most recent call last):
File "<stdin>", line 1, in <module>
NameError: name 'spam' is not defined
>>> '4' + 3
Traceback (most recent call last):
File "<stdin>", line 1, in <module>
TypeError: Can't convert 'int' object to str implicitly
```

The last line the error message gives you will always indicate what happened. There are several types of exceptions. The type is printed in the message. In our sample, the types are TypeError, NameError and ZeroDivisionError. The remainder of the line will provide the detail based on what typed of exception it is and why it happened.

At the beginning of an error message, you will see where the mistake occured. That context will be shown in the form of a stack traceback. It usually will contain a stack traceback listing the lines of code where mistakes were made. However, what you won't see are any lines it read from standard input.

Handling Exceptions

You can write programs that will handle some exceptions. In the next example, you will see the program asking someone for someone to enter a number until the right number is entered, but it will also allow the user to pause the program. In this example, a pause generated by the user is signaled by using the KeyboardInterrupt exception.

```
>>> while True:

    try:

    x = int(input("Please enter a number: "))

    break

    except ValueError:

    print("Oops! That was no valid number. Try again...")
```

Now let's take a look at how the try statement works. The following is a step by step walk through:

1. The statements in the try clause are run.
2. If there is not an exception, the except clause will be passed over and the running of the try statement is done.
3. If there is an exception, the remainder of the clause will be skipped. Then if the exception type matches the exception named after the except keyword, then the except clause will be ran. The execution then will continue following the try statement.
4. If there would be an exception that isn't identical to the exception named in the except clause, then it will be skipped over to other try statements. If there is no handler is found, then it will be an exception that has not been handled and the program will stop with an error message as in the example shown above.

There can be multiple except clauses within a try statement in order to point out handlers for multiple exceptions. At the most, only one handler will be ran.

Concrete Exceptions

Here is a list of some of the commonly raised exceptions and what they mean:

AssertionError: this is given when an assert statement doesn't work.

AttributeError: This execption happens when an attribute reference or assignment stops. If an object doesn't support an attribute reference or an attribute assignment then a TypeError is given.

EOFError: This happens when then input() function comes to an end-of-life condition without reading any data.

FloatingPointError: When a floating point fails, this happens. It is normally shown, but will only come up if you have programmed Python with the –with-fpectl option, or the WANT_SIGFPE-HANDLER symbol becomes defined in the pyconfig.h file.

GereratorExit: This error message comes up if a generator or coroutine ends. It is really not seen as an error and so instead of taking from Exception, it takes from BaseException.

ImportError: When a sequence subscript error goes out of range, Python will show this error.

KeyError: This occurs when a mapping key can't be found.

KeyboardInterrupt: If a user hits the control-c or the delete key, you will see this message. Python checks for interrupts regularly during execution. This exception takes after BaseException so that it doesn't get caught up in the code that catches Exception and prevents the programmer from leaving the program.

MemoryError: If a program has no more memory, but you can rescue it by getting rid of some objects, you will see this message. Python will include a message telling you which operation ran out of memory. That makes it easy for the programmer to track and fix if they can.

NameError: If there is not a global or local name, then it will only apply to unqualified names and is an error message that will tell you which name couldn't be found.

OSError: If there is a system related error, Python will give you this message. That includes I/O failures. An example being "file not found".

Winerror: In windows, this will give you the origional Windows error code. Errno is then a translation of the Windows code.

OverflowError: If the result of a Math operation is too large, then you will see this error. It can't happen for integers, however, this error is sometimes raised for some integers outside of a required range.

RecursionError: This error is like the RuntimeError. It happens when the interpreter determines that the total recursion depth is exceeded.

ReferenceError: This happens when a weakened reference is tries to access attributes of the referents after they have been destroyed or thrown away.

RuntimeError: If an error occurs that doesn't fit into any of the other categories, then this is the error message you will see.

SyntaxError: Given when the program causes a syntax error. It may occur in an import statement, or when using one of the built-in functions, or when Python is running the initial code.

IndentationError: Happens when your indentation isn't done correctly.

SystemError: When the program finds that there is an internal error, but it isn't so bad that the programmer should give up. The message will tell you what went wrong so you can find it.

SystemExit: This exception receives from the BaseException instead of Exception. So it won't be mistakenly caught by the code that catches Exception. If this is not taken care of, the Python interpreter will exit.

TypeError: This happens when you assign a function or operation to a value of the wrong type. You will receive a message giving you details about the mismatch.

UnboundLocalError: If you try to reference a local variable in a method or function, but a value bond to the variable has not been given.

UnicodeError: This error has factors that will tell you about the encoding or decoding error. It is given when Python finds that there is Unicode-related encoding or decoding error occurs.

UnicodeEncodeError: This happens when a Unicode-related error happens while encoding.

UnicodeDecodeError: This happens when a Unicode-related error happens during deciding.

UnicodeTranslateError: This happens when a Unicode-related error happens during translation.

ValueError: When you have built-in operations and they receive and argument with the right type, but using the wrong value, but there isn't a more precise exception for the situation to describe it.

ZeroDivisionError: In a division or modulo operation, if the second argument would have the value of 0, then the value associated with that would be a string showing operands and operation type.

Chapter 8: Tips and Tricks

In this chapter, we will take a look at some tips and tricks for those of you just beginning to use Python. These even may be some things that could be useful to more advanced users. These coding tips are used with Python 2 and Python 3 as these are the two most preferred versions of Python.

#1 Running Scripts

On most UNIX systems you can run Python code from the command line like this:

run python script

$ python MyFirstPythonScript.py

#2 Python Programs from Python Interpreter

The IDLE screen is very easy to learn to use. This is where you can try your first programming steps and later, you can practice codes to see what results you will get. The answer is always immediate as soon as you press enter after typing your code. You can start the console with the command:

start python console

$ python

>>> <type commands here>

#3 The Enumerate() Function

To add a counter to an iterable object, this is the function that you would use. An iterable, gives back an iterator and is an _iter_ method that has an object. It takes indexes in order starting at zero. If something should go wrong in one or more of the indexes, then you would see an IndexError.

One of the most common examples of what the enumerate () does would be to keep track of an index by looping over a list. To do that, you would use a count variable. Python makes it nicer by giving us a syntax for this which is the enumerate () function.

This is what you would enter:

#First prepare your list of strings (Rememer, these are notes to yourself)

Subjects = ('My', 'Python', 'Book')

For i, subject in enumerate(subjects):

Print i, subject

The output would then look like this:

0 My

1 Python

2 Book

#4 Data Type Set

This is a type of collection. It was introduced into Python in version 2.4. A set includes an unordered group of unique and immutable objects. Sets cannot have more than one occurrence of identical elements because they are an implementation of the same <sets> used in Math.

If you would like to make your own set a set, all you'd need to do is use a . Here is an idea of how to create a set with a set of another iteable object along with the set () function and then perform a search in set.

Objects = {'My', 'favorite', 'Python', 'resource', 'book'}

#print set

print(objects)

print(len(objects))

#Use of 'in' keyword.

If 'tips' in objects:

Print('My favorite Python resource book.')

#Use of 'not in' keyword

If 'java book' not in objects:

Print('My favorite Python resource book not java book.')

The output would then look like this:

{'favorite', 'Python', 'resource', 'book', 'beginners'}

5

My favorite Python resource book.

My favorite Python resource book not java book.

Now to start an empty set:

items = set()

#add three strings.

items.add('python')

items.add('resource')

items.add('book')

print(items)

The output would then look like this:

{'Python', 'resource', 'book'}

#5 Dynamic Typing

When you are using Python, you don't have to provide the types of data because Python keeps track of them internally based on what you've typed. That means that

#6 == And = Operators

In Python == is used for comparison. Python also uses = for assignment. In Python, inline assignment is not supported so there is not a chance of mistakenly assigning values when you only want to compare something.

#7 Conditional Expressions

Conditional expressions are allowed in Python. Instead of writing an if.. else with only one variable assignment to each branch, you can do the following if you would want the number to always be off.

#8 Concatenating Strings

In Python, you can use the + if you want to concatenate strings. Here is an example:

>>> print 'Python'+ 'Fun' + 'Tips'

The output would then look like this:

Python Fun Tips

#9 Modules

In order to have your programs stay organized and easy to follow as they get bigger, it may be helpful for you to separate them up into modules. Python will allow you to use modules including many definition types . Then you are able to import your modules so that you can use them in other scripts and programs. You must use a .py extension.

#10 Consistency about Indentation

When you are writing your code in Python, the indention level is very important. It is never a good idea to mix tabs and spaces. If you prefer to use Python 3 it will refuse to read the mixed file.

If you are writing code and you think someone else may read it someday, indentation is so very important because if you aren't using it, the code just becomes messy. Tabs are also very good to avoid because the idea of tabs are just not very well defined and can mean so many different things in the computer world that it can just become confusing. Tabs can end up being destroyed or wrongly converted.

#11 Control your Flow

When you are starting out in Python, learning control structures can be a challenge. It's common to go over for, while, and try-except. These structures can handle just about every case if they are properly used.

Using exceptions as flow control is common when working with databases, files, or any other resources that are likely to fail.

#12 Using Generators

In Python 2, Generators were introduced as a simple way to use an iterator that doesn't hold all of its values at once. Generators are different then functions. Functions usually start the execution, do some operations and then return the result or return nothing.

Instead of using the return keyword, you should use the yield keyword. So rather than getting the result of a function, we see a generator object which you can then use anywhere you could use a list or other iterable. Most often, generators are used as part of a loop.

#13 To use print or print()

This is a Python 2 or Python 3 thing. Throughout this book our examples have been based on Python 3. Almost every developer who has upgraded from Python2 to Python3 has typed the wrong print statement. So it would be good for you to standardize using print as a function by importing print_function.

#14 What version of Python

Often you will find that you use features that aren't available in the older versions of Python. That means that if someone has an older version and they want to use one of your programs, then they will get an error message with an ugly exception traceback. These are not at all helpful, so it's much better to use this:

import sys

if not hasattr(sys, "hexversion") or sys.hexversion < 0x020300f0:

    sys.stderr.write("Sorry, your Python is too old.\n")

    sys.stderr.write("Please upgrade at least to 2.3.\n")

sys.exit(1)

In order to help another user, you should have these lines at the top of your programs. Put them in your program before you type any import statement.

Chapter 9: 10 Special Python Tricks!

In the previous chapter we looked at some tips and tricks for using Python. Now I'm going to add ten special tips and tricks to help you even further!

#1 Easy Sharing

At some point you will want to share files from a directory. You can easily do that by doing this:

Python2

python -m SimpleHTTPServer

Python 3

python3 -m http.server

That would start up a server for you.

#2 Evaluating Expressions

We talked about evaluating expressions in an earlier chapter. We learned about using eval to accomplish this. Now I'm going to share literal_eval. Instead of doing this:

expr = '[5, 6, 7]'

my_list = eval(expr)

You can do this:

Import ast

My_list = ast.literal_eval (expr)

Much easier, right? This has been a part of Python for a few versions, but not everyone has figured it out.

#3 Profiling a Script

If you want to profile a script, you can easily do that by doing this:

Python –m cProfile my_script.py

#4 Breakpoints

You can easily set breakpoints in your script by using the pdb module like this:

Import pdb

Pdb.set_trace()

You can write pdb.set_trace() anywhere I your code to set a breakpoint there. It is super convenient. Pdb also has a few other fun hidden tricks as well.

#5 If Constructs

You can very easily simplify if constructs when you need to check for more than value by doing this:

If n in [7, 8, 9, 10,]

Rather than:

If n==7 or n==8 or n==9 or n==10

#6 To reverse a list or String

If you want to reverse a list, you can do that by doing this:

>>> a = [7, 8, 9, 10]

>>> a[::-1]

[10, 9, 8, 7]

This will quickly create a reverse list. If you want to reverse a list that you have in place, you can do:

a.reverse()

You can also use this method to reverse a string.

#7 Ternary Operators

These operators, or conditional operators, are shortcuts for the if-else statement. You can use them to make your code look more compact and beautiful. Here is an example:

[on_true] if [expression] else [on_false]

x, y = 50, 25

small = x if x < y else y

#8 The Zen of Python

Python's philosophy for you to keep in mind as you code.

The Zen of Python, by Tim Peters

Beautiful is better than ugly.

Explicit is better than implicit.

Simple is better than complex.

Complex is better than complicated.

Flat is better than nested.

Sparse is better than dense.

Readability counts.

Special cases aren't special enough to break the rules.

Although practicality beats purity.

Errors should never pass silently.

Unless explicitly silenced.

In the face of ambiguity, refuse the temptation to guess.

#9 Signal Numbers to Names

At the moment there is not an existing function to convert a signal number over to a signal name. It would certainly be a very nice function to have. So this is the function will help you to accomplish that.

```python
import signal

def signal_numtoname (num):

    name = []

    for key in signal.__dict__.keys():

        if key.startswith("SIG") and getattr(signal, key) == num:

            name.append (key)

    if len(name) == 1:

        return name[0]

    else:

        return str(num)
```

#10 Mixing a Python script and a Shell script

On occasion you may find it very helpful to write code that can be together both in shell and Python at the simultaneously. In shell, a string of four quote characters means a blank empty string. In Python, it begins with a string that is triple quoted and begins with a quote character. Within those strings, you can actually bury shell commands. Keep in mind, that the beginning string in a code is simply there as the document string. Otherwise, Python just ignores it.

Conclusion

I hope that you've enjoyed reading *Python: Fudamental hints and tips to kickstart your Python skills.* I hope that it was informative and able to provide you with all of the tools you will need to achieve your goals both in the near term and in the months and years to come. I have tried to pack this book as full of information as possible to get you started, however there is always more information out there. So remember that to become an expert on something takes time. It is a process and you will grow as you move forward.

The next step is to use what you've learned here and practice. Remember to use IDLE and practice your code because you will get automatic results. While you may be tempted to dive right into Python and try writing programs, take some time to do a little research and learn the short cuts and how each of the different functions work. Which ones will be best for the type of code you are writing. Most of all have fun with Python. That's what its creator had in mind after all!

Finally, if you've enjoyed this book and found it useful in any way, please leave a review on Amazon. It would be appreciated!

www.ingramcontent.com/pod-product-compliance
Lightning Source LLC
LaVergne TN
LVHW052314060326
832902LV00021B/3878